What Do
PULLEYS AND GEARS
Do?

Heinemann
LIBRARY

David Glover

www.heinemann.co.uk/library
Visit our website to find out more information about Heinemann Library books.

To order:
 Phone 44 (0) 1865 888066
Send a fax to 44 (0) 1865 314091
Visit the Heinemann Bookshop at www.heinemann.co.uk/library to browse our
 catalogue and order online.

First published in Great Britain by Heinemann Library,
Halley Court, Jordan Hill, Oxford OX2 8EJ, part
of Harcourt Education. Heinemann is a registered
trademark of Harcourt Education Ltd.

Editorial: Clare Lewis and Katie Shepherd
Design: Victoria Bevan and Q2A Creative
Illustrations: Barry Atkinson (pp5, 17, 21), Douglas Hall
(p6) and Tony Kenyon (p4)
Picture Research: Mica Brancic
Production: Helen McCreath
Printed and bound in China by WKT Company
Limited

10 digit ISBN 0 431 06407 5
13 digit ISBN 978 0 431 06407 9
10 09 08 07 06
10 9 8 7 6 5 4 3 2 1

British Library Cataloguing in Publication Data
Glover, David
What do pulleys and gears do? - 2nd Edition
621.8'3
A full catalogue record for this book is available from
the British Library.

Acknowledgements
The publishers would like to thank the following for
permission to reproduce photographs: Trevor Clifford
pp1, 4, 5, 12, 14-19, 21; Collections/Keith Pritchard
p9; Mary Evans Picture Library p10; Stockfile/
Steven Behr p20; TRIP/H Rogers p13; TSW/ Alastair
Black p7; Zefa/Damm p6.

Cover photograph reproduced with permission of
ImageState/ Stephen Jenkins.

The publishers would like to thank Angela Royston for
her assistance in the preparation of this book.

Every effort has been made to contact copyright
holders of any material reproduced in this book. Any
omissions will be rectified in subsequent printings if
notice is given to the publishers.

The paper used to print this book comes from
sustainable resources.

Any words appearing in the text in bold, **like this**, are
explained in the Glossary

Contents

What are pulleys and gears?

Pulleys and gears are special wheels. They help to make some machines move.

When you turn the crank handle on this model windmill, it makes the sails turn. The handle and the sails are linked by a rubber band. This is the **drive belt**. The drive belt is stretched over two pulleys. It makes both pulleys turn together.

drive belt

pulleys

crank handle

Can you spot the pulleys on this yacht? Pulleys help sailors to raise the sails up the mast. The sailors pull down on ropes on the deck.

The first pulleys

Who invented the pulley? Nobody knows, but the first pulleys were probably just smooth tree branches. Many people must have had the idea of throwing a rope over a tree branch to lift a heavy load high enough to keep it out of the reach of animals, or to put it on a cart.

Cranes and block and tackle

The hook on this crane is fixed to a pulley. A steel rope runs under the pulley, touching its underside. A powerful **motor** winds the rope up and down to raise the load. Other ropes and pulleys move the load to and fro along the arm of the crane. This arm is called the jib.

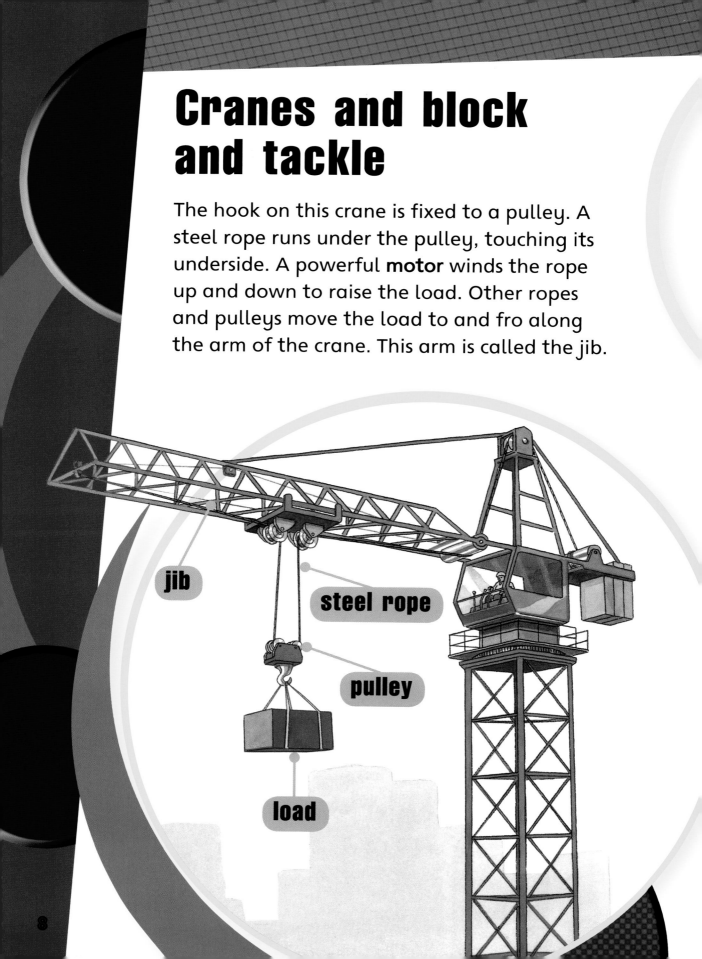

jib

steel rope

pulley

load

This machine crushes sugar cane to extract the juice. It has many moving parts. A steam engine drives it. Drive belts, pulleys, and gears make the parts go round.

Drills, whisks, and reels

When you turn the handle on this drill it makes the drill bit turn at high speed. The drill bit is held in the **chuck**. The handle is linked to the chuck by bevel gears. Bevel gears have sloping teeth. They change the direction in which things turn.

The gear wheel on the handle is much bigger than the gear wheels on the chuck. This means that the chuck goes round several times each time the handle turns once.

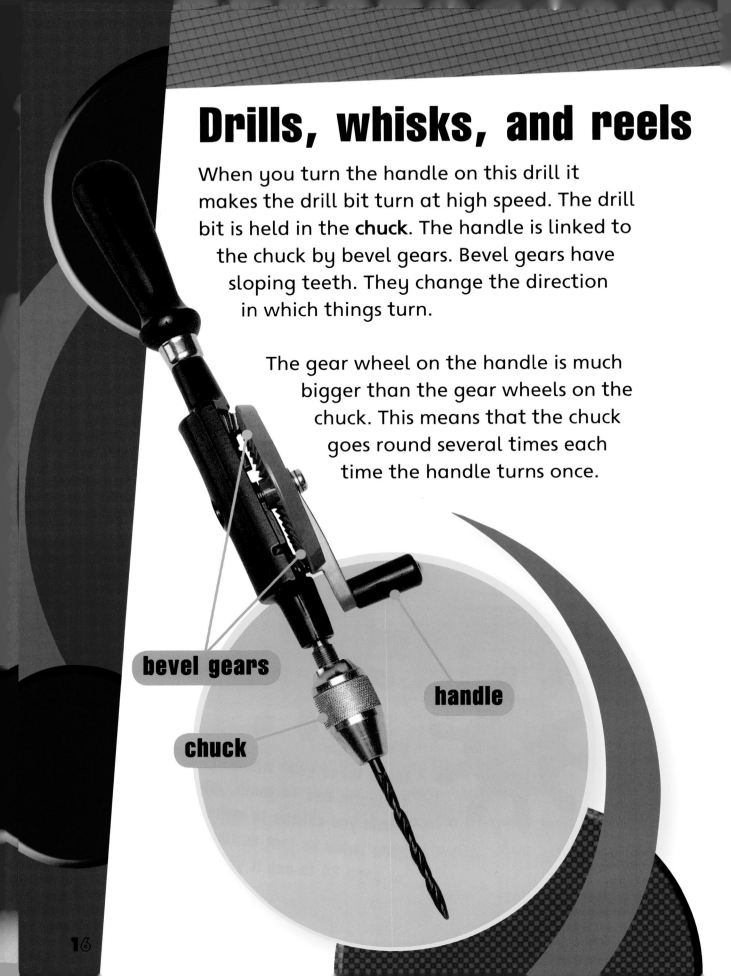

bevel gears

handle

chuck

This whisk has two blades. They are turned by gear wheels on either side of the big gear wheel on the handle. The blades turn in opposite directions, so everything mixes in very well.

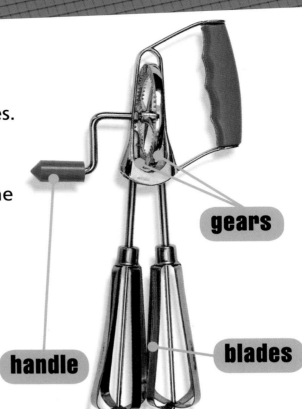

gears

handle

blades

Changing direction

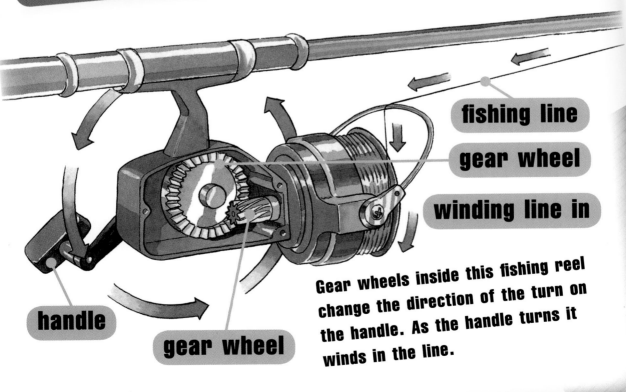

fishing line

gear wheel

winding line in

handle

gear wheel

Gear wheels inside this fishing reel change the direction of the turn on the handle. As the handle turns it winds in the line.

Clocks and watches

The three hands on a clock or watch go round at different speeds. The same **mechanism** turns them all. Each hand is linked to the mechanism by different gears.

During the time the hour hand turns one complete circle, the minute hand turns 12 times. Extra gears help the hour hand go more slowly than the minute hand.

hour hand

minute hand

second hand

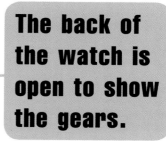

The back of the watch is open to show the gears.

Gears turn the hands of a cuckoo clock. They are powered by falling weights instead of a **motor**. Extra gears turn the parts that make the cuckoo pop out every hour.

Mountain bikes

The chain on a mountain bike fits over the teeth on special gear wheels. These wheels are called **sprockets**. The chain carries the push on the pedals to the back wheel. This push turns the back wheel.

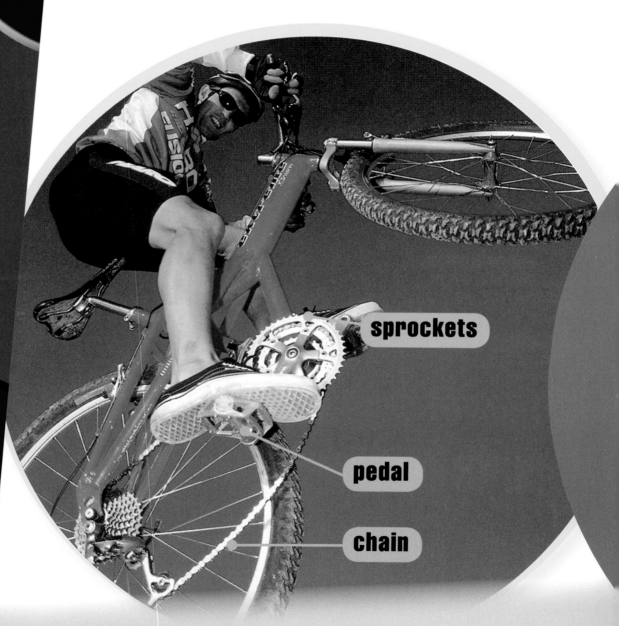

sprockets

pedal

chain

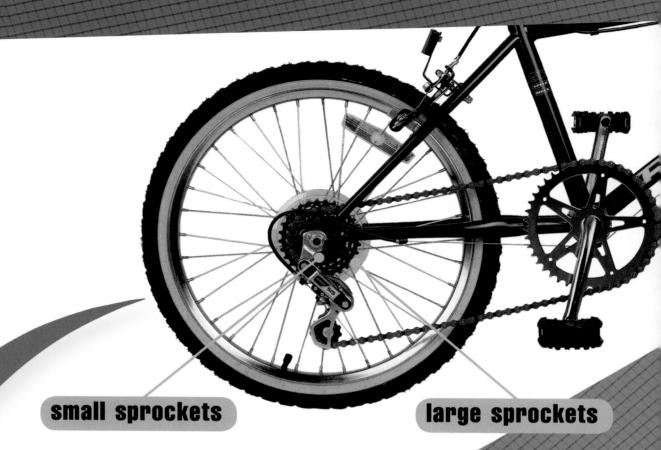

small sprockets

large sprockets

When you change gear on a bike, the chain moves between different sized sprockets on the back wheel. Large sprockets are easy gears for climbing hills. Small sprockets are hard gears for going fast along flat ground.

ELIN	
Z753510	
PETERS	27-Feb-2012
621.83	£10.99

Activities

A simple pulley

1. Tie a long piece of thread or string to a thick book.
2. Use the string to lift up the book.

3. Now put the string over the back of a chair so that the book hangs freely.
4. Pull down on the string to lift up the book.
5. Which way of lifting the book is easier?

See pages 6–7 to find out why.

Gears in action

1. You will need an egg whisk like the one in the photo.

2. Slowly turn the handle and watch what happens.

3. The handle turns the big cog wheel.
4. The big cog wheel turns the two small cog wheels.
5. How many times does each beater go round when you turn the handle once?

See page 11 for an explanation.

Glossary

chuck the part on a drill that grips the different sized drill bits

drive belt loop of leather or rubber that links one pulley wheel to another

gear train series of gear wheels which carry turning movements from one part of a machine to another

mechanism the parts that move together to make a machine work

mesh when the teeth on two gear wheels fit together

motor a machine that uses electricity or fuels such as petrol or coal to make things move

sprockets the toothed wheels on the pedals and back wheel of a bicycle

spur gear flat circular gears with teeth around the edge

steam engine motor or engine which uses steam from boiling water to make things move

worm gear a gear like a screw with a spiral thread running around its surface

Index

The answer to the question on page 15 is:
the 7-toothed wheel goes twice as fast as the 14-toothed wheel.
Were you right?

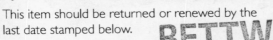

H. G. WELLS : A PICTORIAL BIOGRAPHY

H. G. WELLS
A Pictorial Biography

by Frank Wells

WITH AN INTRODUCTION BY
FRANK SWINNERTON

JUPITER BOOKS

First published in 1977 by
JUPITER BOOKS (LONDON) LTD
167 Hermitage Road, London N.4

SBN 904041 22 0

Composed in Monotype Bembo, Series 270,
by Kelly & Wright, Bradford-on-Avon, Wiltshire

Printed and bound in Great Britain by
R. J. Acford Limited, Chichester, Sussex.

PREFACE

This is a Family Album of Photographs, slightly and lightly added to. It includes a Parallel of Events to give some indication of what others were doing at the time that he was growing up and teaching and writing and living. But I have tried to do no more than take the contents of a box in the attic and put them in some sort of order. Do not take it too seriously — just enjoy it.

F.J.W.

Contents

FRANK SWINNERTON

INTRODUCTION

I remember with pleasure the fact that when I first saw H. G. Wells he had just published, and I had just read, his exciting venture into world prophecy, *Anticipations*. This was in the year 1901, and I was reception clerk in the showroom of J. M. Dent & Co., publishers. Although Dents were famous for their reprints of the classics they had also produced, with enterprise but only modest success, a number of modern novels, among which were two very early works by Wells, *The Wonderful Visit* (1895) and *The Wheels of Chance* (1896). It may have been with the object of recovering rights in these books that the author made his call. If it was, he failed.

He came very briskly into my domain, asked to see Mr Dent (who had a habit of not seeing difficult customers), and turned away to examine the bookshelves covering the walls above and beside a large open fire. I had no more than a glimpse of the mischievously roving blue eyes, and was chiefly impressed by an enormous travelling overcoat such as prosperous men then wore. He was quick, courteous, and anxious to depart as soon as possible. I doubt if he saw J. M. Dent that day, because my recollection is that in a few seconds he was gone, leaving me with the thrill of having been in contact with a man of extraordinary vitality. It was a great day in my young life.

Eight or nine years later I sat just behind Bernard Shaw and Arnold Bennett in an audience at the Times Book Club to which Wells read a most stimulating paper, afterwards reprinted in *An Englishman Looks at the World,* on 'The Contemporary Novel'. It was a defence, not only of his own large scale, all-embracing fiction, but of a form which was already suffering from the attacks of those who insist that fact is more important to humanity than work of the imagination; and it illustrated a strong Wellsian characteristic—his generosity to other writers. Conrad, Bennett, and the author of *Elizabeth and Her German Garden* were all highly praised. Flaubert's

Bouvard et Pecuchet was extolled. The novel was rated above biography, autobiography, and history, since these other literary forms 'can hardly ever get beyond the statement that the superficial fact was so. It is by comparison irresponsible and free. Because its characters are figments and phantoms, they can be made entirely transparent.

The paper was a great success. Although the reader confessed his faults as a public speaker, and although his voice lacked resonance, he delighted his audience and did splendid work for the novel by justifying its existence in an increasingly political world. At the same time an attack was made upon Henry James's limited conception of it as a sort of easel picture, with 'foreground', 'middle distance', and, above all, 'form'. James was a master of form; Wells regarded it as a species of cramp. The reason for this was that he had been much lectured about 'art' by James, Ford Madox Ford, and Edward Garnett, to whom Turgenev was a god.

I was then a beginning novelist, whose boyhood had been spent among poor people, and whose books, accordingly, dealt with such people, especially in the nearer suburbs of London. I had neither literary friends nor a scholastic background; but through the enforced solitude of illness I had read much and developed a critical habit. Knowledge of my work led Martin Secker, then a very new publisher, to suggest that I should write for him a study of the work of George Gissing. I knew, as yet, nothing about Gissing, and all my efforts to obtain personal information regarding his life and character were vain. I was therefore compelled to estimate the man by drawing inferences from his books and from such printed comments as were available.

My 'study' was published in the autumn of 1912; and the next thing I knew was that a most enthusiastic review of it appeared in an 'advanced' periodical called *Rhythm,* conducted by John Middleton Murry, Katherine Mansfield, and Michael Sadleir. The review was by Wells; and it was followed by an invitation to Sunday supper at the Wells home in Hampstead.

This was an astonishing experience. The party was a large one, including William Rothenstein, the artist; Henry Arthur Jones, the elderly dramatist; and H. C. Marillier, who managed the decorative art firm established by William Morris. We supped with decorum; but after the meal we trooped upstairs to a long room on the first floor, where, to the accompaniment of a pianola, the entire company cast dignity aside, assumed fancy robes and headgear (Henry Arthur Jones wore an upturned brass flowerpot), and pranced rather than danced until exhaustion and helpless laughter led to chairs and a flow of talk. In these activities Wells was the most agile; but Mrs Wells was his equally energetic partner. I had never been to such a party; but I pranced and laughed as the others did; and even earned praise for my performance.

I have said that Mrs Wells was as energetic as her husband. Born Amy Catherine Robbins, but 'Jane' to all close friends, she was small, pale, quiet, and amazingly resourceful. Arnold Bennett once described her as 'a great woman'; and this would be my own verdict also. At a first unperceptive encounter one might have noticed only a tiny voice and a subdued manner; but she was lion-hearted, a splendid housekeeper and hostess who saw everything that passed and made sure that everybody was happy. It was she who did much of the research for *The Outline of History*. It was she who typed the Wells manuscripts and helped to correct the proofs. If Wells cut his finger, or a guest was injured in one of the many games of hockey or lawn tennis which were essential to Wells's love of action, it was she who acted as doctor and nurse. When music was needed at a rehearsal of some amateur theatricals I have seen her sit down to the piano and play with brio. And, with it all, she had a loving heart and a sympathy in which I never saw any trace of sentimentality. Altogether, as Arnold Bennett said, 'a great woman'.

From that evening in 1912 I was constantly an invited guest, at first to large parties in, I think, Queen Anne's Mansions, and, after the family removal to a former rectory in Essex which was re-named Easton Glebe, for weekends. The weekends involved a houseful of visitors, who ranged from professors to playwrights, from journalists to M.P.s, from Charlie Chaplin to young men from Cambridge University who were friends and fellow-students of the two Wells boys. All were free to come and go; but if they came they joined in the round of activities and made new friends at every visit. Arriving for the most part on Saturday afternoon by train from London, they were met by car and driven through Lady Warwick's park to the house. There, in a magnificent long room, panelled in what I now recall as a warm biscuit colour, they were made welcome.

At table there was always good talk, led by H. G. himself. Except that sometimes Philip Guedalla arrived with witticisms which had been long pondered, the flow of conversation was entirely spontaneous. Fun was made of grave figures; tales were told of past episodes or recent events in the different worlds frequented by Wells and the visitors; and never at any time did anybody feel that we were in the company of a man of worldwide renown. Indeed, Wells never saw himself as such a man. Though his public quarrels were notorious, he was essentially modest. It was not of his reputation that he was jealous; it was of his ideas that he was tenacious. He wanted to bring about a commonwealth in which men and thoughts were free.

This led to some amusing incidents. Once, when I was spending a weekend with Sir Harry Johnston, who had been Governor of Uganda, always dressing for dinner whatever his surroundings, and combining the utmost fearlessness with Victorian ideas of decorum, I found him still agitated by the memory of a recent visit from H. G. He had proposed a prim engagement in that most vicious of back lawn games, croquet; but hoops and posts had no attraction for his guest. The whole of a very large garden became a field of play. All rules were abandoned. What should have been a cosy bout of small tricks and skills developed into a steeplechase. This was entirely characteristic. Wells thought in cosmic terms.

His energy, which I first noted as briskness, was insatiable. Immediately after breakfast on Sunday morning, the party was led to a great barn in the garden, where a large soft ball was struck by hand backwards and forwards over a high net, with many a cunning ricochet from a dropped part of the ceiling. The game over, it was Wells who led the less exhausted players to the tennis court. In winter crowds of local residents arrived for hockey, to meet the Wells brigade and be run off their feet. And, after all, Wells would ask those he loved 'What other game can we play, that I can win?'

I have said 'those he loved'; and this brings me to another outstanding trait, his capacity for real affection. He had other, and more publicised, associations; but these were outside my personal knowledge, although once, when we were walking together without companions, he remarked confidentially: 'Much worse than the worst is known about me, Swinny.' What I have in mind is the kindness he showed, not only to myself, but to many more. He took strong likings; he encouraged young talent; and he wrote generously, and talked very merrily, about his rivals in the public eye. As a controversialist he did not shine as a guiding light; he was unscrupulous and sometimes insulting, as when, in exasperation at over-zealous lectures urging discipline from Henry James, he likened that subtle writer's art to the work of a hippopotamus picking up a pea. But the insults were always due to his cascading sense of the ridiculous, or comic inventiveness. Irreverence, in his case, did not affect a much deeper admiration. Once, when he and I were talking of the James brothers, and I spoke highly of William, whom I knew he greatly esteemed, he said 'Oh, but Henry was by far the greater man'.

He thought quickly, and his thoughts covered a wide range of subjects and ideals. The books he wrote illuminate the range; and his quickness drove him to endless supplements and revisions for as long as printers could be persuaded to send him proofs. It was true, as Henry James insisted, that his novels tended to sprawl as no works of pure art should do. They did this from the fertility of their author. They did not meander; they grew.

As I now think of them, and of Wells himself, it is with admiration of his ebullient genius and affection for one who never failed in kindness and generous praise for an obstinate junior. I recall that when I wrote a book which was poorly received by English reviewers he secretly wrote an introduction to the American edition which completely changed its fortunes in that country. This was a bold and deliberate act of warmheartedness.

It was characteristic. Wells helped to mould his age; but he was first of all young Bert, the boy who had listened disrespectfully and with a keen ear for ridiculous colloquialisms, to gentlemen's gentlemen at Uppark, where his mother was housekeeper. He then became the shop assistant and student who experienced the difficulties of Art Kipps (curiously enough, several of Art's mishaps had in reality befallen Jane) and the misadventures of Mr Lewisham. And, finally, he was the irrepressibly inventive humorist to whom ideas for comic or astounding short stories came flying upon every breeze. Although his enthusiasm for a society dominated by 'plain living and high thinking' inspired idealists all over the world, he never forgot Uppark and the tiny villa in Claygate where he and Jane first lived, when their budget was so small that he seriously considered 'selling' his whole literary output to a publisher for three hundred pounds a year. If he appeared fleetingly in one of his own books, it was as 'little Wilkins, the novelist'.

This was the H. G. who was loved by his friends. Other successful men have kicked away past associations as they ascended the social scale and attained celebrity. He did nothing of the kind. Brimming with fun, as indeed were his contemporaries Bernard Shaw, Gilbert Chesterton, and Arnold Bennett, he communicated to others a fine zest for life, and he kept them amused to the end, not only by his genius, but because, like Art Kipps, he was 'a simple soul'. His simplicity, as well as his many-sidedness, will be found represented in the present volume.

FRANK SWINNERTON

H. G. WELLS : A PICTORIAL BIOGRAPHY

1864 Jules Verne published *Voyage to the Centre of the Earth*
Foundation of First Ladies Public Boarding School, Cheltenham
1865 National Society for Women's Suffrage (John Stuart Mill)
1866 Prussia and Italy attack Austria
H. G. Wells born
1867 Birth of Arnold Bennett and John Galsworthy
Marx pub. *Das Capital*
1868 February: Disraeli P.M.
December: Gladstone P.M.
1869 Darwin pub. *Variations in Animals*
Jules Verne pub. *20 thousand Leagues under the Sea*
1870 Franco-Prussian War
Death of Dickens
T. H. Huxley pub. *Lay Sermons*
1871 Surrender of Paris
Darwin pub. *The Descent of Man*
1872 Bertrand Russell born
1873 Jules Verne pub. *Around the World in Eighty Days*
Founded: Girton, first College for Women attached to Cambridge University

At four-thirty in the afternoon of 21 September 1866 Herbert George Wells was born at 47 High Street, Bromley, Kent, 'blasphemous and protesting'. Immediately behind No. 47 there was a slaughterhouse so the noise in that part of Bromley must have been considerable.

His mother, Sarah Neal, was lady's maid at Uppark near Midhurst, where she met Joseph Wells, son of the head gardener at Penshurst Castle.

They married in 1853 and in 1855 moved into Atlas House, a china shop, No. 47 High Street, Bromley. Joe was a bad shopkeeper but a good professional cricketer. In 1862 he took four wickets with four consecutive balls playing for Kent against Sussex.

BROMLEY ACADEMY,

In Union with the College of Preceptors,

BROMLEY, KENT.

PRINCIPAL—THOMAS MORLEY, L.C.P. *(Exam.)*

Late Member of the Council. Author of "A help to memory in Book-keeping" in a sheet.

The object of Mr. Morley's Academy is to prepare Youth for the various Mercantile and Professional pursuits and the success of the Middle Class Examinations of the College of Preceptors, London, which has attended pupils from the school, unmistakably establishes the character of instruction imparted.

The acquisition of the French language is facilitated by the intercourse between the French and English pupils.

References to Parents, whose sons have been educated by Mr. M., may be had on application.

The Course of Instruction comprehends—LANGUAGES: English, French, and Latin.—HISTORY: English, Modern and Ancient, including Biblical History, with especial reference to Ancient Egypt.—GEOGRAPHY: Sacred and Secular.—Plain and Ornamental Writing, Arithmetic (logically), Booking-keeping, Mensuration, Algebra, Euclid, Trigonometry, Plane and Spherical; Mechanics, Conic Sections, Differential and Integral Calculus, and Chemistry. **TERMS MODERATE.**

School will Re-opened on Tuesday, January 11th, 1876.

Young Bertie went to Bromley Academy in 1874 and left there in 1876.

H. G. said of this school: 'I had certainly acquired the ability to use the English Language with some precision and delicacy . . . but . . . he crippled my French for life. . . .'

1874 Birth of G. K. Chesterton
1875 Employers & Workers Act
     Public Health Act
     Women admitted to Trade Union
     Congress
1876 Victoria becomes Empress of
     India
     Watson and Bell first 'voiced the
     Telephone'
1877 Russo-Turkish War
1878 Treaty of Berlin
1879 Lady Margaret Hall and Somerville
     College founded at Oxford
     Birth of Stalin
1880 Gissing pub. *Workers in the Dawn*
     Franchise conferred on Women
     in the Isle of Man
     Aerated Bread Company opened
     first Tea Shops in London
1881 Foundation of *The Evening News*
1882 Death of Darwin
1883 Death of Karl Marx

In 1877, after an accident, Joseph Wells had to give up cricket and the china shop
became bankrupt. In 1880 Sarah Wells returned to Uppark as Housekeeper.

H. G. Wells' first known manuscript story, written and illustrated about 1879 and published in 1957.

Rodgers & Denyers 25 High Street
Sunday July 4th 1880

My dear Mother
Here I am sitting in my bed room after the fatigues of the day etc Cough slightly better & I am tolerably comfortable
I give you an account of one days work to give you an idea what I have to do.
Morning
We sleep together viz 3 apprentices & 1 of the hands in one room (of course in separate beds)
We lay in bed until 7.30 when a bell rings & we jump up & put trousers slippers socks & jacket on over nightgown & hurry down & dust the shop etc
about 8.15 we hurry upstairs & dress & wash for breakfast.
At 8.30 we go into a sort of vault underground (lit by gas) & have breakfast
after breakfast I am in the shop & desk till dinner at 1 (we have dinner underground as well as breakfast) & then work till tea (which we have in the same place) & then go on to supper at 8.30 at which time work is done & we may then go out until 10.30 at which time the apprentices are obliged to be in the house
I don't like the place much food it is not at all like home
Give love to Dad & give the Cats my best respects
I'm rather tired of being indoors but ...

In 1880 Bertie was first apprenticed to a Draper in Windsor and from there he wrote this letter to his mother.

I went to Clewer Church & then on to Surley which I found much better than I used to think it in fact its a perfect heaven to R...
I'm rather tired so excuse further writing
yours H G Wells
NB My washing will be 1/- a quarter

Below Stairs at Uppark. At this kitchen Table Bertie started his career as a journalist, editing the Uppark Alarmist.

Rodgers & Denyers decided he was unsuited to become a Draper, so he took a job as a pupil teacher at Wookey in Somerset, in a school run by 'Uncle Williams', who was not a properly qualified teacher so the school had to close, and Bertie was again without occupation. He became a Chemist's Assistant in Midhurst and was dismissed for breaking too much glass and fighting the porter. From 1881–1882 he was again apprenticed to a Draper—in Southsea. He implored his Mother to help him return to teaching although she would have to pay his keep for a year—altogether £35.

This is the Science Lab. at Midhurst Grammar School: from there H. G. won a 'Teacher in Training' Scholarship to the Normal School of Science, in 1884.

Taught by T. H. Huxley, H. G. said *I believed then he was the greatest man I was ever likely to meet, and I believe that all the more firmly today.*

The Normal School of Science in 1885, now the Royal College of Science, South Kensington.

T. H. Huxley and Julian Huxley in 1885. Many years later Julian Huxley, H. G. and G. P. Wells worked together on *The Science of Life*.

In 1887 he got a second-class degree and failed in the final examination in Geology. He returned to teaching; first at Holt Academy near Wrexham, and in 1889 at Henley House School in London, run by J. V. Milne, who allowed him enough time to study for another go at an Honours B.Sc.

In 1890 H. G. took first-class Honours in Zoology and first place in second class Honours in Geology.

J. V. Milne with his three sons, Barry and Ken and seated, A. A. Milne

1884 Foundation of the Fabian Society
1885 Birth of D. H. Lawrence
1886 Foundation of 'Science Schools Journal'
Henry James pub. *The Bostonians*
Thomas Hardy pub. *The Mayor of Casterbridge*
R. L. Stevenson pub. *Dr Jekyll & Mr Hyde*
1887 Frank Harris revived 'The Fortnightly Review'
1888 H. G. pub. *The Chronic Argonauts*
Death of Matthew Arnold
1889 Birth of Adolph Hitler
Bernard Shaw pub. *Fabian Essays in Socialism*
1890 William James pub. *Principles of Psychology*

Between pages 11 and 12
1891 Kipling pub. *The Light that Failed*
H. G. pub. *The Rediscovery of the Unique* in the Fortnightly Review
1892 Kipling pub. *Barrack Room Ballads*
Death of Tennyson
1893 Foundation of the Independent Labour Party
Oscar Wilde pub. *Lady Windermere's Fan*
Conan Doyle pub. *Memoirs of Sherlock Holmes*
1894 The Dreyfus Affair
Kipling pub. *The Jungle Book*
1895 Joseph Conrad pub. *Almayer's Folly*
Stephen Crane pub. *The Red Badge of Courage*
Death of T. H. Huxley
The Oscar Wilde Case

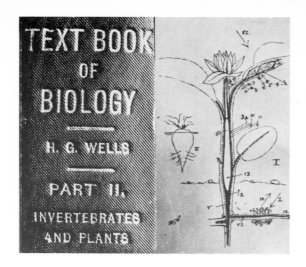

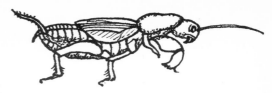

Gryllotalpa, the mole cricket.

In 1886 H. G. founded and was first Editor of 'The Science Schools Journal', and knowing the Editor can be a distinct help in getting into print. In that year he published *Talk with Gryllotalpa*.

H. G. was also writing prolifically in the 'Saturday Review', the 'Fortnightly Review', 'Gentleman's Magazine', 'Pall Mall Gazette', 'Nature', 'Chamber's Journal', the 'New Review' and others.

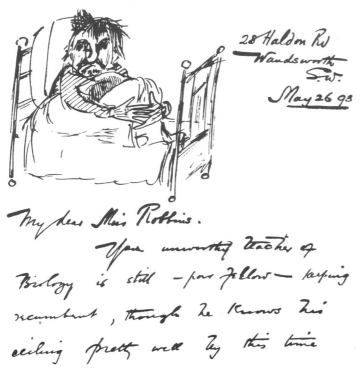

28 Haldon Rd
Wandsworth
S.W.
May 26 93

My dear Miss Robbins.

Your unworthy teacher of Biology is still — poor fellow — keeping recumbent, though he knows his ceiling pretty well by this time

Isabel Mary

With an Honours Degree he got a reasonably well paid job with the University Correspondence College. In 1891 he married his cousin Isabel Mary and they lived in Wandsworth. The marriage was not a success and they separated three years later.

    First Published Books: (1893) *Text Book of Biology*, 2 vols.
                         Honours Physiography with R. A. Gregory

In 1895 he published *Select Conversations with an Uncle, The Time Machine, The Wonderful Visit, The Stolen Bacillus and Other Stories*

They lived in:
1895 'Lynton', Station Rd., Woking
1896 'Heatherlea', Worcester Park
1898 Beach Cottage, Sandgate, Kent
1899 Arnold House, Sandgate

He published:
1896 The Red Room
     The Island of Doctor Moreau
     The Wheels of Chance
1897 The Plattner Story & others
     The Invisible Man
     Certain Personal Matters
     Thirty Strange Stories
1898 The War of the Worlds
1899 When the Sleeper Wakes
     Tales of Space & Time
     (Oscar Wilde described H. G. as
     'a scientific Jules Verne'.)

In 1893 he had met Amy Catherine Robbins and found in her 'the embodiment of all the understanding and quality I desired in life'. In 1894 they lived together in Mornington Place and in Mornington Street. They married when free to do so in 1894.

Neither of them liked the christian name 'Amy'; H. G. called her 'Jane'.

H. G. photographed by Jane

Jane

H. G. photographed by Jane

Jan 14/99

Waiting for the Verdict.

Poor stuff!

Sketch by H. G.

1896 Foundation of the *Daily Mail*
1897 Queen Victoria's Diamond
     Jubilee
     Conrad pub. *Nigger of the
     Narcissus*
     Somerset Maugham pub. *Liza of
     Lambeth*
1898 Oscar Wilde pub. *The Ballad of
     Reading Gaol*
     Bernard Shaw pub. *Plays
     Pleasant & Unpleasant*
     Kitchener conquers Sudan
1899 The Boer War
     E. Nesbit pub. *The Treasure
     Seekers*
     Kipling pub. *Stalky & Co.*
     Birth of Jorge Luis Borges

All his manuscripts, letters and business
were done for him by Jane on a
Remington.

In 1897 Pearson's Magazine published an article entitled THE OUTPUT OF AUTHORS. The contributors to these 'interesting Confessions of Popular Writers' included Hall Caine, Conan Doyle, Rider Haggard, Cutliffe Hyne, Max Pemberton, William le Queux, and H. G. Wells who said:

Heaven alone knows how much I write on an average; but on an average I burn half at least of what I write—the net product is not more than 1000 words a day. I like thinking about my stories, but I hate writing them; the only things that are pleasant to write are essays (but they are not nearly so pleasant to sell) and malignant criticism of my contemporaries.

For six months or more, when I was scrambling for a footing amongst novelists, I must have turned out, Heaven forgive me! about 7000 words each working day; 'Moreau' and 'The Wonderful Visit' came in that feverish time, and there were theatrical criticisms, and book reviews, and copious articles, and the beginning of a novel that was a bother even to burn. I hope some day to give two years to a book, and to be able to burn it at the end if I do not like it. No novelist can do his best work until he feels free to do that.

In 1900 they built Spade House at Sandgate in Kent. Designed by C. F. A. Voysey for an H. G. who, on medical advice, expected to live his few remaining years in a wheel-chair. Before the house was finished dormer windows and nurseries were built into the roof. H. G. and Jane forgot ill-health and planned a family.

The Sitting Room at Spade House

Frank Wells (seated) and G. P. Wells

The Rolling Stock, Engines, Lines and Points were all made by H. G.'s brother, Frank.

In Spade House H. G. wrote and published :
1900 *Love & Mr Lewisham*
1901 *The First Men in the Moon*
Anticipations
1902 *The Discovery of the Future*
The Sea Lady
1903 *Mankind in the Making*
Twelve Stories & a Dream
1904 *The Food of the Gods*
1905 *A modern Utopia*
Kipps
1906 *In the Days of the Comet*
The Future in America
Faults of the Fabian
Socialism & the Family
1907 *The So-called Science of Sociology*
The Misery of Boots
Will Socialism Destroy the Home?
1908 *New Worlds for Old*
The War in the Air
First & Last Things

Jane and H. G.

Joseph Conrad

H. G. Wells and camera

VISITORS TO SPADE HOUSE
Between 1900 and 1905 H. G. and Jane took these Photographs

George Bernard Shaw

W. Pett Ridge

1 Sept. 1900

My Dear Bennett,
What will you give us if we don't send
you your photograph? We haven't
printed it yet but the negative looks
good for a fiver to me.
                    Yours Ever
                    H. G. Wells

George Gissing

Joseph Wells and his three sons: Frank the clockmaker, Freddie the Draper from Jo'burgh, and Bertie the writer.

Shaw and Wells

Conrad and Wells

Sidney Olivier and his beautiful Daughters with H. G.

AS M. FONTAINE SAW IT: M. BLÉRIOT'S LANDING AT DOVER.

DRAWN BY OUR SPECIAL ARTIST, S. BEGG, FROM DETAILS SUPPLIED BY M. FONTAINE.

THE LANDING OF A CONQUEROR ON DOVER CLIFFS: M. BLÉRIOT ALIGHTING ON ENGLISH SOIL AFTER HIS CROSSING
OF THE CHANNEL BY MONOPLANE.

M. Fontaine, who most courteously supplied our Artist with the details for this drawing, is the French journalist who chose the landing-place for M. Blériot and signalled its whereabouts to
the daring aviator by waving a tricolour flag. As soon as he saw that M. Blériot had seen the flag he waved against the white face of the cliffs, M. Fontaine, still carrying the tricolour, ran
as fast as he was able towards the meadow. M. Blériot passed him, and, after circling once or twice, landed some sixty or seventy yards from him.

H. G., Hugh Popham, Jimmy Horsnell, Mrs. Popham, and Jane. Jimmy was
H. G.'s secretary and later a dramatic critic who wrote under the initials H. H.

1900 Boer War
     Boxer Rising
     Conrad pub. *Lord Jim*
1901 Death of Queen Victoria
1902 Bennett pub. *Grand Babylon
     Hotel*
     Conrad pub. *Youth*
     End of Boer War
     First Post Office Telephone
     Exchange in London
1903 H. G. joins the Fabian Society
     Samuel Butler pub. *The Way of all
     Flesh*
     Conrad pub. *Typhoon*
     Death of Gissing
1906 H. G.'s first visit to U.S.A.
1908 First Old Age Pensioners Act
1909 Bleriot flies the Channel

H. G. published:
1909 *Tono Bungay*
     Ann Veronica
1910 *The History of Mr Polly*
1911 *The New Machiavelli*
     The Country of the Blind & *other
     stories*
     Floor Games
     The Door in the Wall & *other
     stories*

In 1909 H. G. moved from Spade
House to 17 Church Row, Hampstead,
and in 1911 to Essex.

The lead soldiers that H. G. used in the War Game are still in use, owned, repaired and repainted by his great-grandsons.

In 1911 H. G. rented Little Easton
Rectory from Lady Warwick and later
bought the House and Land and changed
its name to Easton Glebe. The square
block is the original house and the bay on
the left is part of the additions that H. G.
added a few years later.

'It was a square looking old red brick house he had come to, very handsome in a simple Georgian fashion, with a broad lawn before it and great blue cedar trees . . .
'Breakfast was in the open air, and a sunny easy-going feast. Then the small boys laid hands on Mr Direck and showed him the pond and the boats.'
(*Mr Britling sees it Through*)

First Motorcar—an Overland

THE MAD DOG OF EUROPE.

THE KAISER GETS HIS ANSWER FROM BRITAIN.

MOBILISATION.

APPEAL FOR AID FROM KING OF THE BELGIANS.

BRITAIN WILL NOT SEE HIM CRUSHED.

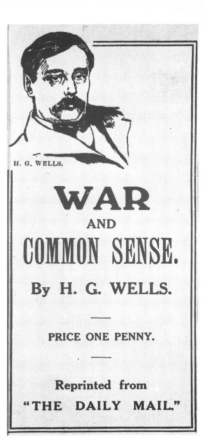

H. G. WELLS.

WAR
AND
COMMON SENSE.

By H. G. WELLS.

PRICE ONE PENNY.

Reprinted from
"THE DAILY MAIL."

Kurt Bütow.
May 1914.

4 August 1914

'The familiar scene of life was drawn aside, and War stood unveiled. "I am the Fact," said War, "and I stand astride the Path of Life. I am the threat of death and extinction that has always walked beside life, since life began. There can be nothing else and nothing more in human life until you have reckoned with me." ' (*Mr Britling sees it Through*)

Lady Warwick's Easton Lodge became a convalescent home for officers. Every Sunday afternoon many of them came to the Glebe and played mixed hockey.

'He nodded his head towards the German Tutor. "Look at that pleasant person. There he is—echt Deutsch—if ever anything was. Look at my son there! Do you see them engaged in mortal combat? The thing's too ridiculous." ' (*Mr Britling sees it Through*)

BRITISH AIRMEN ATTACK AND DAMAGE ZEPPELIN

The Daily Mirror

CERTIFIED CIRCULATION LARGER THAN ANY OTHER PICTURE PAPER IN THE WORLD

No. 3,608   Registered at the G.P.O. as a Newspaper   TUESDAY, MAY 18, 1915   **16 PAGES**   One Halfpenny.

LANDING TROOPS AT THE DARDANELLES: FLEET'S BIG GUNS KEEP THE TURKS AT BAY WHILE OUR MEN GET ASHORE.

Australians landing on the Gallipoli Peninsula. The Commonwealth troops have displayed magnificent bravery against very heavy odds.

Shrapnel bursting over the Turkish troops which were opposing the landing of British forces from the transport on the left of the picture.

These striking pictures have just arrived from the Dardanelles, and show how our men were landed. There will be much heavy fighting before the Allies can hope to reach the Turkish capital, but the early operations give good hope for success, and the enemy losses are already reported to be very heavy. Great Britain has always ex-

celled at amphibious warfare, and the landing of a great army is a task that few nations could undertake. The guns of our warships, however, are able to keep the enemy at bay until the men get a firm footing on shore. Without the fleet the men would be driven back into the sea.

French Chasseurs on the way to the Front

THE FIRST TANK ENGAGEMENT: A BRITISH TANK (ON THE LEFT) FIRING AT A GERMAN TANK, WHICH WAS COMPLETELY "KNOCKED OUT" AT VILLERS-BRETONNE

The first action between Tanks took place near Villers-Bretonneux on April 24, when the German Tanks made their début on the battlefield. The result was a victory for the British Tanks. Six of the enemy's machines accompanied his infantry, and some of our heavy Tanks soon arrived to engage them, and succeeded in driving them off. Presently some of the new British light Tanks, called "whippets," appeared on the scene, and wrought great execution among the German infantry with their machine-guns, seven Tanks manned by twenty men putting 400 Germans out of action. In the drawing a German Tank is seen on the right in the background, while the British machine in the left foreground is firing at it. Further to the left among the trees are British infantry. At the end of the duel the German was knocked out on the right of it, where shrapnel is bursting in the trees, are German troops advancing. The enemy's Tanks are of a somewhat square design, with a gu in front and machine-guns at the sides and rear. The conning-tower is also square in shape. According to correspondents, both British and French, who have German Tanks, they are ineffectively armoured, and the range of vision ahead from the conning-tower is impeded by defects of design.

In 1903 H. G. had published in the Strand Magazine *The Land Ironclads* which
described steam-driven machines which bear, in essentials, a remarkable resem-
blance to the tanks of 1916.

In the peaceful Essex Gardens the guns from the Western Front could be heard, and the pheasant woke and warned the approach of Zeppelins, hearing them long before we humans could.

'Colour had returned to the World, clean pearly colour, clear and definite like the glance of a child or the voice of a girl, and a golden wisp of cloud hung in the sky over the tower of the Church. There was mist upon the pond, a soft grey mist not a yard high. A covey of partridges ran and halted and ran again in the dewy grass outside his garden railings. The partridges were very numerous this year because there had been so little shooting. Beyond in the meadow a hare sat up as still as a stone. A horse neighed . . . Wave after wave of warmth and light came sweeping before the sunrise across the world of Matching's Easy. It was as if there was nothing but morning and sunrise in the world. (*Mr Britling sees it Through*)

In 1920 he went to Prague and was received by President Masaryk. He was able to see much of the new Czechoslovakia.

Then he visited Lenin in Russia, stayed with Maxim Gorky and shopped for plates from the ex-Imperial Porcelain Factory.

H. G. with his host, Maxim Gorky, and interpreter Moura Budberg.

Frank Swinnerton extreme left, Phillip Guedalla third from the right.

Mr Britling says, 'The two small boys became active in the garden beating in everybody to dress up before supper.' At the time of this photograph they were at Cambridge and Easton became increasingly invaded by undergraduates. In spite of this H. G. wrote and published *The Outline of History* in 1920, brilliantly illustrated by Frank Horrabin, seen below with his wife.

George Bernard Shaw, Hilaire Belloc and G. K. Chesterton

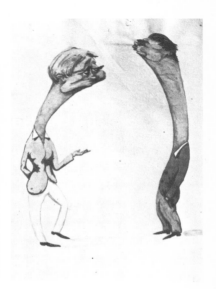

Here are the two sons as seen by the eldest; and below is his cartoon of Phillip Guedalla.

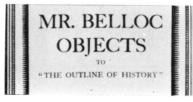

MR. BELLOC
OBJECTS
TO
"THE OUTLINE OF HISTORY"

H. G. Wells as seen by Low.

	Mrs. Milne			Mrs Laski	
Harold Laski	St. John Ervine	Charles Chaplin	H. G. W.	Mrs Byng	Mrs Ervine
G. P. W.					
Hugh Cranmer Byng		F. R. W.			A. A. Milne

When Chaplin came to Easton for a weekend one of the other guests was Harold
Laski, who looked much more like Chaplin than did Chaplin, as Laski had a
small moustache. A number of locals lined the hedge at the end of the garden to
catch a glimpse of Chaplin. H. G. took Laski for a walk on the lawn and the
spectators went away satisfied.

A GREAT RUSSIAN SINGER IN LONDON:
M. CHALIAPIN INTERESTED IN JEWELLERY.

H. G. gave a party at Whitehall Court for Chaliapin to meet Charlie Chaplin.
It was a great success—but neither Chaliapin nor Chaplin turned up.

TO THE ELECTORS OF LONDON UNIVERSITY GENERAL ELECTION, 1923, FROM H. G. WELLS, B.Sc. (Lond.)

DEAR SIR OR MADAM,

The fantastic action of Mr. Baldwin in precipitating the country into another General Election within a year of the last one obliges me to follow up my recent communication to you with a formal election address.

In that previous letter I placed my general views people's views of the way in which Great Britain is to meet the tragic crisis of vanished employment that the decadence of Central Europe, through the obstinacy of M. Poincaré's Government and the empty weakness of Mr. Baldwin's, has brought upon great masses of our workers. Our country has never been a self-subsisting country. Several

In 1922 and in 1923 he stood for parliament as a Labour Candidate. He was not elected.

with the best wishes for 1924
to Mr & Mrs WELLS
from the Low family

1920 Hitler founds National Socialist
Party
1921 Harding president of U.S.A.
Washington Conference on
Naval Disarmament
1922 Conservatives win Election
1923 Coolidge president of U.S.A.
Conservatives lose Election
1924 Death of Lenin
Conservatives win Election
1925 Treaty of Locarno
Mein Kampf
1926 General Strike

Lloyd George and H. G. Wells

1. E. F. Benson
2. H. M. Tomlinson
3. W. Somerset Maugham
4. W. W. Jacobs
5. A. P. Herbert
6. T. F. Powys
7. John Buchan
8. Maurice Baring
9. Beverley Nichols
10. A. A. Milne

11. Compton Mackenzie
12. J. D. Beresford
13. Bernard Shaw
14. Arthur Bryant
15. Philip Guedalla
16. Harold Nicolson
17. J. Middleton Murry
18. Havelock Ellis
19. Herbert Read
20. Philip Gibbs

21. Humbert Wolfe
22. Laurence Binyon
23. John Drinkwater
24. Walter de la Mare
25. Siegfried Sassoon
26. G. K. Chesterton
27. Clemence Dane
28. Helen Simpson
29. V. Sackville-West
30. Henry Handel Richardson

31. Rose Fyleman
32. E. V. Lucas
33. Rebecca West
34. Hugh Walpole
35. Charles Morgan
36. Aldous Huxley
37. Sir Arthur Quiller-Couch
38. J. B. Priestley
39. H. G. Wells

Key to the portraits of "A Literary Levée," reproduced on the cover;
specially designed and photographed by Howard Coster.

H. G. lived at Easton from 1911 until 1929, from Peace through the 1914–1918
'War to end War', until the death of his wife in 1927, when the house became
empty and lifeless.

AMY CATHERINE WELLS (JANE)
died on 6 October 1927

'. . . she managed to sustain her belief that I was worth living for, while I made my way through a tangle of moods and impulses that were quite outside her instinctive sympathy. She stuck to me so sturdily that in the end I stuck to myself. I do not know what I would have been without her. She stabilised my life. She gave it a home and dignity. She preserved its continuity. Not without incessant watchfulness and toil. I have a hundred memories of an indefatigable typist carrying on her work in spite of back-ache; of a grave judicial proof-reader in a garden shelter, determined that no slovenliness shall escape her. . . .' *The Book of Catherine Wells*

In the years 1911–1929, while at Easton,
    H. G wrote:
The Great State
The Labour Unrest
Marriage
War & Commonsense
Liberalism & its Party
Little Wars
The Passionate Friends
An Englishman looks at the World
The World Set Free
The Wife of Sir Isaac Harman
The War that will End War
The Peace of the World
Boon
Bealby
The Research Magnificent
What is Coming?
Mr Britling sees it Through
The Elements of Reconstruction
War & the Future
God the Invisible King
A Reasonable Man's Peace
The Soul of a Bishop
In the Fourth Year
Joan & Peter
British Nationalism & the League
The Undying Fire
The Idea of a League of Nations
The Way to a League of Nations
History is One
The Outline of History
Russia in the Shadows
The Salvaging of Civilisation
The New Teaching of History
Washington & the Hope of Peace
The Secret Places of the Heart
The World, Its Debts & Rich Men
A Short History of the World
Men Like Gods
The Story of a Great Schoolmaster
The Dream
A Year of Prophesying
Christina Alberta's Father
A Forecast of World Affairs
The World of William Clissold
Mr Belloc Objects
Democracy Under Revision
Meanwhile
The Way the World is Going
The Open Conspiracy
Mr Bletsworthy on Rampole Island
The Book of Catherine Wells
The King who was a King
The Common Sense of World Peace
The Autocracy of Mr Parham
The Science of Life (with Julian Huxley
    & G. P. Wells)
& other pamphlets, articles & so on

Some of it in this Garden Study,
designed by that gifted charlatan,
Frank Wells.

H. G. at the B.B.C., 1929

1928 Sale of Easton Glebe
Move to Chiltern Court
Aldous Huxley pub. *Point
Counterpoint*
D. H. Lawrence pub. *Lady
Chatterley's Lover*
Women get the Vote at 21
1929 Hemingway pub. *Farewell to Arms*
Priestley pub. *The Good
Companions*
R. C. Sherriff pub. *Journey's End*
Second Labour Government
Wall Street Collapse; World
Slump
1930 Evelyn Waugh pub. *Vile Bodies*
Deaths of Conan Doyle and D. H.
Lawrence
1931 Spain becomes a Republic
Death of Arnold Bennett
F. D. Roosevelt president of
U.S.A.
Conference of Lausanne (War
Debts)
Conference of Geneva
(Disarmament)

When H. G. was considering taking a flat in Chiltern Court, a block built over
the very busy Baker Street Station, he asked the Landlords if they could convince
him that he would have no disturbance from the noise and vibration of the Trains.
He was advised that he could rest assured of the quiet suitability of the flats for a
writer as Arnold Bennett had just taken one.

When Arnold Bennett made the same enquiry he was told that H. G. Wells
had just taken a flat there.

H. G. published:
1931 *The Way to World Peace*
What are we to do with Our Lives?
*The Work, Wealth & Happiness of
Mankind*
1932 *After Democracy*
The Bulpington of Blup
*The Queer Story of Brownlow's
Newspaper*
1933 *The Shape of Things to Come*
1934 *Experiment in Autobiography*
Stalin—Wells Talk

H. G. with Sir John Lavery at the Premiere of the Paul Robeson Film 'Emperor Jones', 1934.

1935 *The New America, The New World*
Things to Come (Film story)
1936 *The Anatomy of Frustration*
The Croquet Player
The Idea of a World Encyclopaedia
Man who could Work Miracles (Film)
1937 *Star Begotten*
Brynhild
The Camford Visitation
The Informative Content of Education

WHAT ARE WE TO DO WITH OUR LIVES?

By

H. G. WELLS

❡ A revised and re-written edition of Mr. Wells' "The Open Conspiracy."

❡ It contains <u>an answer</u> to the present crisis in human affairs and <u>a workable plan</u> for the way out.

3s. 6d.
NET

Book-jacket, 1931

'Bluppery', 1932

At the Commission of Enquiry into the Reichstag Trial by World Lawyers, London, 1933.

1933 Nazis take power in Germany
Deaths of Galsworthy and George
Moore
H. G. leaves Lou Pidou and re-
turns to England

H. G. with Pavlov

1934 He visits President Roosevelt and Joseph Stalin, and also visited Pavlov at Koltushy

With best wishes for a
merry Christmas ~
a happy New Year.
Theodore Roosevelt
Eleanor B. Roosevelt.

H. G. with Alexander Korda, 1935.

SAVOY HOTEL,
OCTOBER 13TH,
1936.

P. E. N.
Birthday Dinner
TO
H. G. WELLS.

1936 H. G. Wells' 70th Birthday

J. B. Priestley presided at the celebration dinner. Here he, Mrs Priestley and H. G. welcome the guests.

Now that he is seventy, an Interlude to see how other people saw H. G. In the early 1920s his son G. P. Wells saw him like this:

The Artist's Father.
about to write a Book.

H. G. Wells.

It is interesting to note that G. P. W. emphasises the forward-swelling brow—which in 1926 David Low also observed.

And as seen by Jo Davidson, an American Sculptor working in Paris.

And this one by an unknown artist who had perhaps never seen H. G. The impression given that the work is by H. G. Wells was presumably intentional, but rest assured that H. G. had no interest or faith in Palmistry.

And this is how David Levine saw Him.

Once again David Low, an unfinished and unpublished drawing.

It is well worth while looking at the marginal detail more closely.

To return to our story . . .
In 1937 H. G. again visited the U.S.A.

Playing ball on board ship.

He is seen with Paulette Goddard.

Merry Xmas.
Paulette
and love.

H. G. visited the U.S.A. in 1906, 1921, 1934, 1935, 1937 and 1940.

With Henry Ford and with Shirley Temple.

H. G. Wells planting an evergreen tree (Arbor Vitae) at the Deering Library, North Western University, Evanston, Ill., 31 October 1937.

From 1936 to 1946 he lived at 13 Hanover Terrace, Regent's Park.

1937. President Educational Science Section, British Association, to whom he read a paper on 'The Informative Content of Education'.

PHOTOGRAPH BY S. ALTSON PEAR

H. G. WELLS MEETS A DUCK-
BILLED PLATYPUS.

In 1939 he visited Australia and in 1940 the U.S.A.

1939. Mosley addresses a meeting in East London, sporting a black shirt as was worn by Mussolini's Fascisti.

H. G. Published:
1938 *The Brothers*
World Brain
Apropos of Dolores
1939 *The Holy Terror*
Travels of a Republican Radical
The Fate of Homo Sapiens
The New World Order
1940 *The Rights of Man*
Babes in the Darkling Wood
The Common Sense of War & Peace
All Aboard for Ararat
1941 *Guide to the New World*
You Can't be too Careful
1942 *The Outlook for Homo Sapiens*
Science & the World Mind
Phoenix
A Thesis
The Conquest of Time
1943 *Crux Ansata*
1944 *42 to 44, A Contemporary Memoir*
1945 *The Happy Turning*
The Mind at the End of its Tether

"The Immediate Future of Mankind"

A Lecture By

H. G. Wells

Presented At

TOWN HALL Opera House San Francisco

November 8, 1940

Dr. Alexander Meiklejohn Chairman.

1940. Daylight Raid on Camden Town

A PENGUIN SPECIAL

What are we fighting for?

H. G. WELLS

ON

THE RIGHTS OF MAN

33. **Weber, Editha,** 27.10.05 Düsseldorf, Erzieherin, vermutl. England, RSHA IV E 4.
34. **Weber, Ludwig,** 22.5.02 Pfungsstadt/Darmstadt, RSHA IV A 1, IV A 2.
35. **Wechselmann, Kurt,** 3.2.88 Mieckobitz, Kaufmann, zuletzt: Den Haag, vermutl. England, RSHA IV E 4, Stapoleit Breslau.
36. **Weck, Kurt,** 20.11.92 Werdau/Sa., vermutl. England, RSHA IV A 1 b.
37. **Weckel, Kurt,** 15.3.77 Schedewitz, Volksschullehrer, RSHA IV A 1 b.
38. **Weogwood, Josiah Clement,** 1872, brit. Oberst, RSHA VI G 1.
39. **van Weegen, Wilhelm,** 1.2.04 Ueden/Holland, zuletzt: Renkum b. Arnheim, vermutl. England, RSHA IV E 4.
40. **Weidmann, Friedrich Wilhelm,** 8.11.02 Erlangen, Arbeiter, London, RSHA II B 3, Stapo Nürnberg.
41. **Weil, Hans, Dr.,** 1905 geb., Assistent, Emigrant, Newcastle-on-Tyne, RSHA III A 1.
42. **Weiler, Gerhard, Dr.,** 1899 geb., Emigrant, Oxford, RSHA III A 1.
43. **Weinberger, Martin, Dr.,** 1893, verh., Emigrant, London, Dozent a. d. Universität, RSHA III A 1.
44. **Weinhart, Josef,** 17.6.97 Gfell, Glan Y Mor, Y. M. G. A., Barry i. Glam, RSHA IV A 1 b.
45. **Weinmann, Fritz,** Emigrant (Jude), London, RSHA III D 4.
46. **Weinmann, Hans,** Hauptaktionär d. Westböhmischen Bergbauaktienvereins, London, RSHA III D.
47. **Weinstein, Alexander, Dr.,** geb. 1897, London, Privatdozent a. d. Universität, Emigrant, RSHA III A 1.
48. **Weisenfeld, Nathan,** Arzt, London, RSHA IV A 2.
49. **Weiß, Bernhard,** 30.7.80 Berlin, ehem. Pol.-Vize-Präs., RSHA IV A 1, VI G 1.
50. **Weiß, Harry, Dr.,** 1906 geb., Emigrant, London, RSHA III A 1.
51. **Weiß, Joseph, Dr.,** 1905 geb., London, Emigrant, Assistent an der Universität, RSHA III A 1.
52. **Weißenberg, Karl, Dr.,** 1893 geb., Emigrant, a. o. Professor, Southampton, RSHA III A 1.
53. **Weizmann, Chaim,** 1873 oder 1874 in Motyli bei Pinks, Professor der Chemie, Führer der gesamten Judenvereine Englands, London S. W. 1, 104 Pall Mall, Reform-Club, RSHA II B 2, VI G 1.
54. **Welker, Helene,** 13.12.04 Berlin, RSHA IV A 2.
55. **Wells, Herbert George,** 1866 geb., Schriftsteller, London N. W. 1, Regents Park 13, Hanover Terrace, RSHA VI G 1, III A 5, II B 4.
55a **Welsh,** brit. N.-Agent, zuletzt: Kopenhagen, vermutl. England, RSHA IV E 4.
56. **Welter, Charles Joseph Ignace Marie,** 6.4.80 Den Haag, ehem. holl. Kolonialminister, zuletzt: Den Haag, Statenplein 10, RSHA III B.
57. **de Werdestuyn, de Wijkersloot, Robert,** 31.9.12 Utrecht, Student, zuletzt: Nymwegen, vermutl. England, RSHA IV E 4, Stapoleit Düsseldorf.
58. **Wenzel, Johann,** Deckname: **Hermann** und **Bergmann,** 9.3.02 Niedau, Schlosser, Schmied, RSHA IV A 2.
59. **Werner, Heinz, Dr.,** 1890 geb., Cambridge, Emigrant, a. o. Prof. an der Universität, RSHA III A 1.
60. **Werner, Hermann,** 27.9.93 Buckwa, vermutl. England, RSHA IV A 1 b.
61. **Werner, Paul Robert,** 16.5.15 Scheidelwitz, Gefreiter, RSHA IV E 5, Stapoleit Breslau.
62. **Wertheimer, Lydia,** Mitarbeiterin d. Merton, London, RSHA III D.
63. **West, Rebeca,** 1892 geb., Journalistin, RSHA VI G 1.

At the time of the expected Invasion (1940) H. G., quite rightly suspecting that he was a marked man on the Nazi lists, had many private letters destroyed, thinking that the writers might be compromised by their association with him. Among the letters were all those from Rebecca West.

[91]

1940. Mussolini, a leader of great energy and slight scruples, inspects his troops. And Hitler inspects his. The World had slid into a war that Hitler had planned.

Ralph Richardson in 'Things to Come', made seven years earlier.

In 1942 H. G. gained his Doctorate of Science.

A THESIS ON THE QUALITY OF ILLUSION
IN THE CONTINUITY OF THE INDIVIDUAL
LIFE IN THE HIGHER METAZOA, WITH
PARTICULAR REFERENCE TO THE
SPECIES HOMO SAPIENS

Submitted by

H. G. WELLS

B.Sc. 1890, with first class honours in Zoology and second class in
Geology, Member of Convocation, for the degree of D.Sc.

1943 The Fall of Mussolini

You are masochist — there
is no other word for it. Still
you must have your way.
For goodness sake keep
quiet for a bit & dont go
stumping all over the house
on your crutches. Eighty
is going well here & I get
better & better & better
Bless you.

H. G.

Letter from H. G. to George Bernard
Shaw when Shaw fell and broke a leg
in his garden, having fallen off a ladder.

D-Day Landings in Normandy—1944.

Opening a series of Talks for Discussion Groups—'Reshaping Man's Heritage'—in B.B.C. Home Service, 15 January 1943.

'42 TO '44

A CONTEMPORARY MEMOIR UPON HUMAN BEHAVIOUR DURING THE CRISIS OF THE WORLD REVOLUTION

'The acquisitive fool with his money bags, the priest with his prayers and incantations, the straining girl in the factory, even the lad in the stokehold of the labouring ship or behind the tommy-gun, can do nothing against our ultimate supreme enemy, Ignorance. Knowledge or extinction. There is no other choice for man.'

This is an Angry Dadda

To Frank & Peggy

This is my expressive photograph to show how Granfer Wells feels about the exploitation of the Under Dog by all the smart Alecs of Reaction.

Gurrrrr!

H. G. was mild in person but, with his pen, vituperative.

THE HAPPY TURNING

A DREAM OF LIFE

Lord Snow (centre) looking at a G.L.C. Plaque which he unveiled on the wall of 13 Hanover Terrace, Westminster, where H. G. Wells lived for the last 10 years of his life. With Lord Snow are H. G. Wells' sons, Frank (left) and Philip. In the background is Mr. J. I. Kagarlitsky, editor of the Russian volumes of Wells's works.

SOME BOOKS ABOUT H. G.

H. G. Wells. A Bibliography, Dictionary & Subject Index
by Geoffrey H. Wells   1926

H. G. Wells—a sketch for a portrait
by Geoffrey West   1930

Experiment in Autobiography by H. G. Wells   1934

H. G. Wells—A Biography by Vincent Brome   1951

H. G. Wells & his Family by M. M. Meyer   1956

The Early H. G. Wells by Bernard Bergonzi   1961

H. G. Wells. A Comprehensive Bibliography
compiled by the H. G. Wells Society   1966

H. G. Wells. His Turbulent Life & Times
by Lovat Dickson   1969

H. G. Wells et son temps by Jean-Pierre Vernier   1971

The Time Traveller by Norman & Jeanne MacKenzie   1973

H. G. Wells. Early writings in Science & Science Fiction
Edited by Robert Philmus & David Y. Hughes   1975

INDEX